MW01358240

Little Eco Experts

Ways to Buy Green

Translated by
Diana Osorio

How to be guardians of the planet

PowerKiDS press

Published in 2023 by PowerKids, an Imprint of Rosen Publishing
29 East 21st Street, New York, NY 10010

Cataloging-in-Publication Data
Names: Editorial Sol 90 (Firm).
Title: Ways to buy green / by the editors at Sol90.
Description: New York : Powerkids Press, 2023. Series: Little eco experts Includes glossary and index.
Identifiers: ISBN 9781725337244 (pbk.) ISBN 9781725337268 (library bound)
ISBN 9781725337251 (6pack) ISBN 9781725337275 (ebook)
Subjects: LCSH: Shopping--Environmental aspects--Juvenile literature. Sustainable living--Juvenile literature. Environmentalism--Juvenile literature.
Classification: LCC GE195.5 W397 2023 DDC 640.28'6--dc23

Coordination: Nuria Cicero
Editor: Alberto Hernández
Editor, Spanish: Diana Osorio
Layout: Àngels Rambla
Design Adaptation: Raúl Rodriguez, R studio T, NYC
Project Team: Vicente Ponce, Rosa Salvía, Paola Fornasaro
Scientific Advisory Services: Teresa Martínez Barchino

Imaging and Infographics:
www.infographics90.com
Firms: Getty/Thinkstock, AGE Fotostock, Cordon Press/Corbis, Shutterstock.

Manufactured in the United States of America

CPSIA Compliance Information: Batch #CSPK23. For Further Information contact Rosen Publishing, New York, New York at 1-800-237-9932.

CONTENTS

What Is Consumption? 4
Consumption Has Two Faces 6
A Product Has a Life? 8
The Eco Backpack 10
Did You Know? 12
Organic Food 14
Transgenic Food 16
From the Field to the Basket 18
Labels Speak Volumes 20
Packaging Is Important 22
Avoid Plastic 24
Fair Trade 26
Sustainable Fashion 28
Which Clothes Are Sustainable? 30
Suitable Toys 32
Responsible Consumption 34
Make Your Own Soap 36
Glossary 40
Index 40

WHAT IS CONSUMPTION?

Consumption is what we spend every day to buy all kinds of things, such as food, clothes, toys, a bus trip, or even your home's electricity.

A Necessary Wheel

Consumption is an economic process necessary to sustain today's society. Take a look at the example of milk consumption. It looks simple, right? Look at how many stages there are in milk consumption, from milking a cow to the purchasing phase, until reaching you.

A Necessary Wheel... ...Keeps Production Active

Cow Milking

Storage

Processing and Bottling

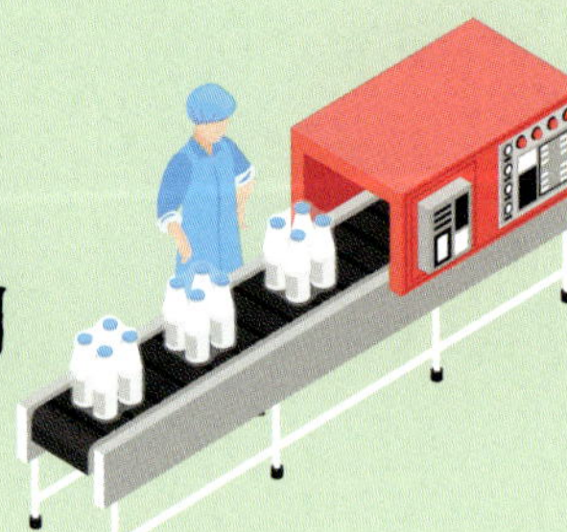

Production and Consumption

The people who produce things receive a payment in return, which is used to pay the employees or providers, or to cover their needs. Consumption keeps production alive.

CONSUMPTION HAS TWO FACES

With Purpose and Care

Consumption is not bad, but we must learn to consume only what we really need, so that our purchase or consumption has a purpose.

Consume with Care

Each Day

All the things we buy or pay for are part of our consumption. Consumption is part of the economy; your city's, your country's, and the world's. Keep that in mind!

Every Day and Everywhere

Today's society encourages us to buy many times more than what we need. For some people, consuming can become an obsession.

Thinking Green!

The well-being of humanity, the environment, and the performance of the economy depend on the responsible management of the planet's natural resources. Therefore, think green! It's much better if you buy products that respect the environment— products that have been manufactured using sustainable standards.

A PRODUCT HAS A LIFE?

Believe it or not, the life of a product—or the things we consume—includes all the necessary processes for its creation. This includes the product's entire useful life and even the stages to later eliminate or recycle it.

A Simple Can Is Not So Simple

You have already seen what the production of milk for consumption entails. Now take a look at a more elaborate and complex product, like a soda can. Have you ever thought about it?

A Product's Lifetime

1 Bauxite is extracted. This mineral is used to make aluminum.

9 The empty can is thrown in a container for cans.

10 At the reycling plant, these are sorted and pressed.

11...

The aluminum is recasted so it can be reused.

2

Metal is melted.

3

Metal is transformed into large cans.

4 **Cans are produced and the brand is printed.**

5 **These are then packed and prepared for transportation.**

6 **They are transported to their points of sale.**

7 **Stores stock them for the public.**

8 **The cans are bought to drink their contents.**

THE ECO BACKPACK

The ecological backpack of a product is the sum of all the materials used in its life cycle, from its creation until it is recycled or disposed of as waste.

It's Better If It Is Light

The lower the weight of a product's ecological backpack, the less harmful it will be to the environment.

So Much in a Backpack!

The products that we consume daily are way more than what we see. What we don't see weighs more than what we do see from the product. Take a look at the amount of pieces that are produced and used to equip a car. We only mentioned a few as examples; a lot more materials are used to manufacture a car.

It's Better If It Is Light

A car's ecological backpack weighs more than 14 tons (more than ten times the weight of the car on its own).

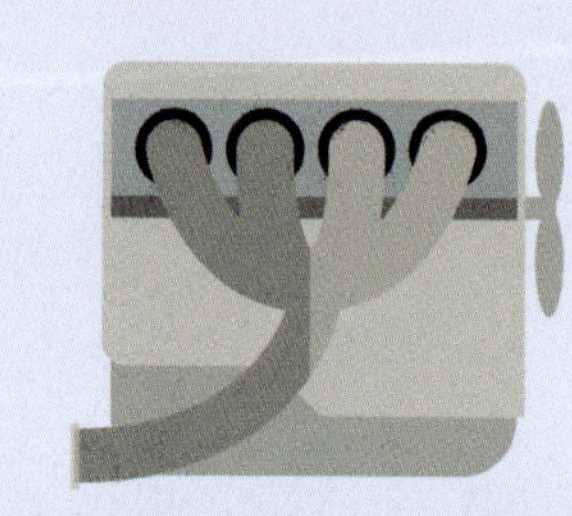

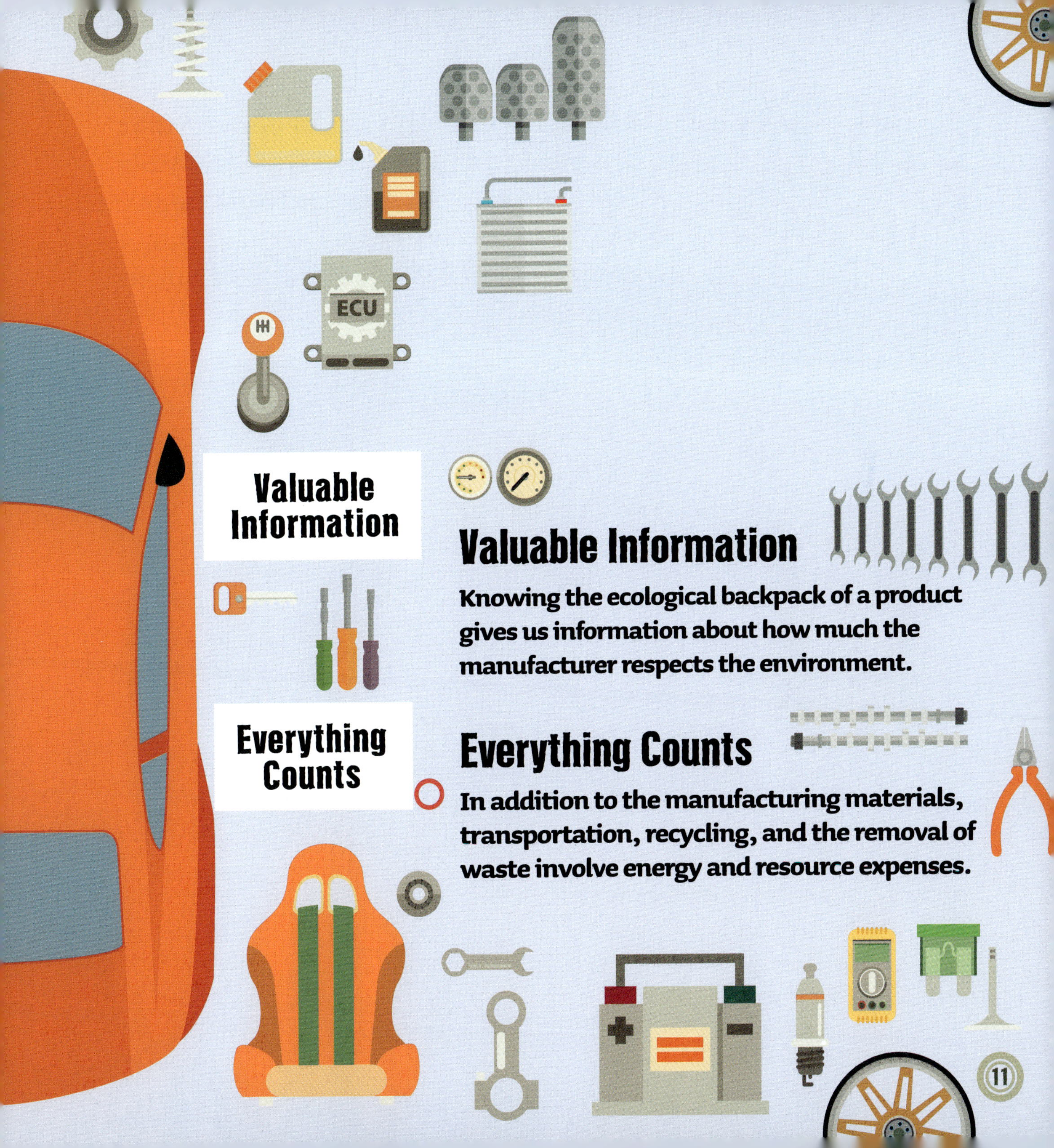

Valuable Information

Knowing the ecological backpack of a product gives us information about how much the manufacturer respects the environment.

Everything Counts

In addition to the manufacturing materials, transportation, recycling, and the removal of waste involve energy and resource expenses.

Valuable Information

Everything Counts

DID YOU KNOW?

About 165 pounds (75 kg) of materials are used to make a smartphone. How many mobile devices are there near you? Do you think they respect the environment? What about computers? And cars?

Regular adult backpack

44
pounds

Smartphone

165
pounds
(3.75 backpacks)

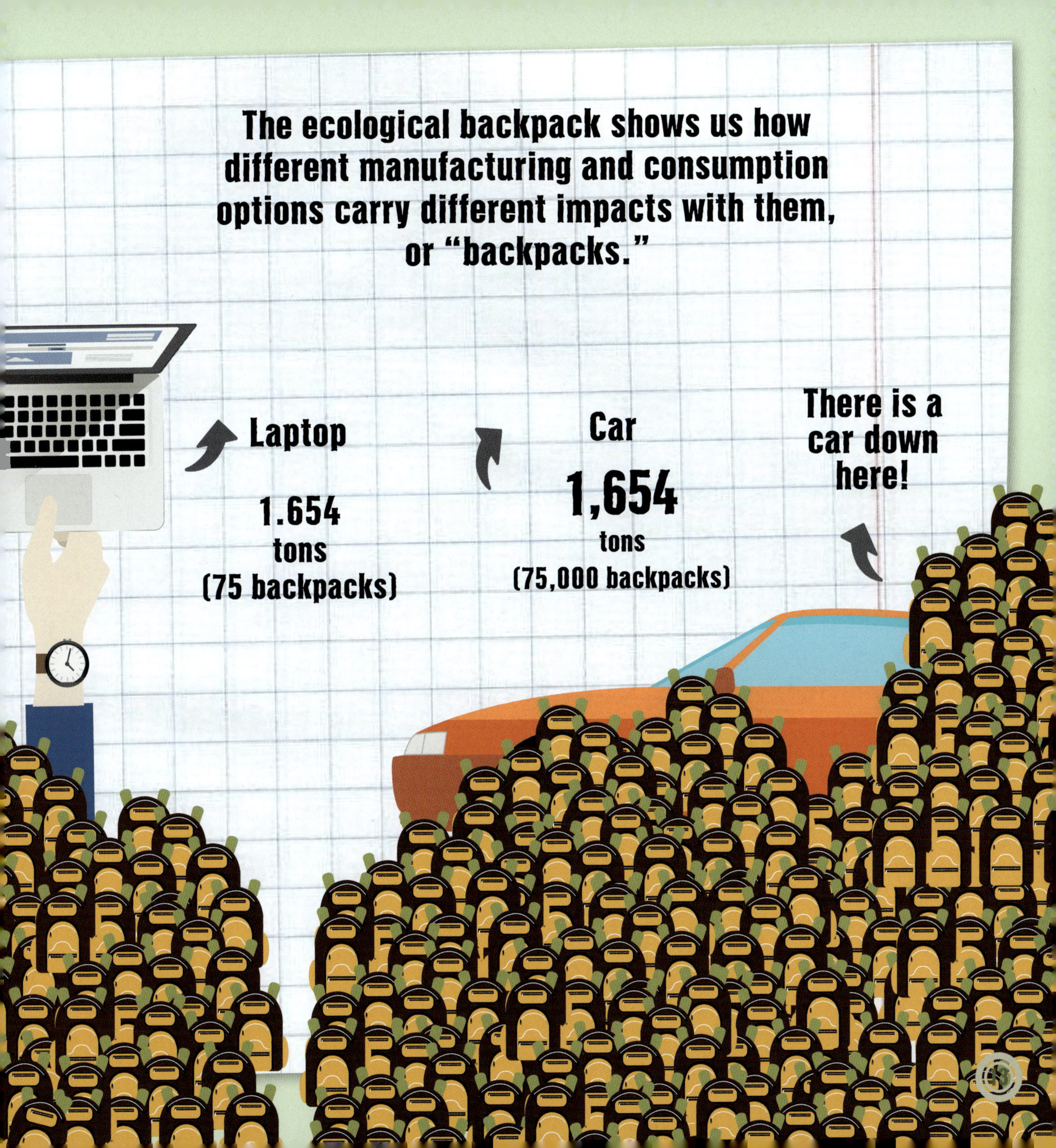

The ecological backpack shows us how different manufacturing and consumption options carry different impacts with them, or "backpacks."
Laptop
1.654 tons (75 backpacks)
Car
1,654 tons (75,000 backpacks)
There is a car down here!

ORGANIC FOOD

Organic foods are those that are produced completely naturally, without chemicals and without damaging or altering the environment.

It is Natural, Above All

Organic farming does not use pesticides or chemical fertilizers that pollute the water and that can be harmful to our health.

Seasonal

Ecological foods are seasonal. In other words, they're typical for an area's climate and the particular time of year.

Be Careful with Packaging

A product is not fully ecological if its packaging isn't. It is best if we buy it by weight and use our own shopping bag.

Ecological Livestock

As well as crops, farm animals can also be ecological. Ecological animals are raised in open environments and fed from ecological products.

TRANSGENIC FOOD

Transgenic foods are obtained from the manipulation of their genes. This modification aims to develop more resistant and productive products. But transgenic foods have pros and cons.

Pros: More Resistant Species

Plant genes are modified in a lab to create more resistant species that grow a lot faster.

More Resistant Species

Helps Fight Hunger

Possibly Helps Fight Hunger

Increased production and more resistant foods could help solve problems of hunger around the world.

Cons: Possible Negative Effects on Health

Although little is known about how transgenic foods affect people's health, they could be negative in the long term, perhaps causing allergies or intolerance to certain foods.

Possible Negative Health Effects

Decreases Biodiversity

Many companies grow crops without taking the rest of the ecosystem into account. The stronger crops overtake the area's original plant life.

Decreases Biodiversity

FROM THE FIELD TO THE BASKET

Greenhouse

Here plants are transplanted to protect them from frost.

Fertilizer

Natural fertilizer is used to make land more fertile.

Other Plants

Other plants are grown in the same area that are beneficial for tomato growth.

Nettles

These are used to repel insects that destroy fruits.

Traditional Crop

Look at the differences between the traditional way of growing tomatoes and the transgenic cultivation of these plants. Which do you think respects nature the most?

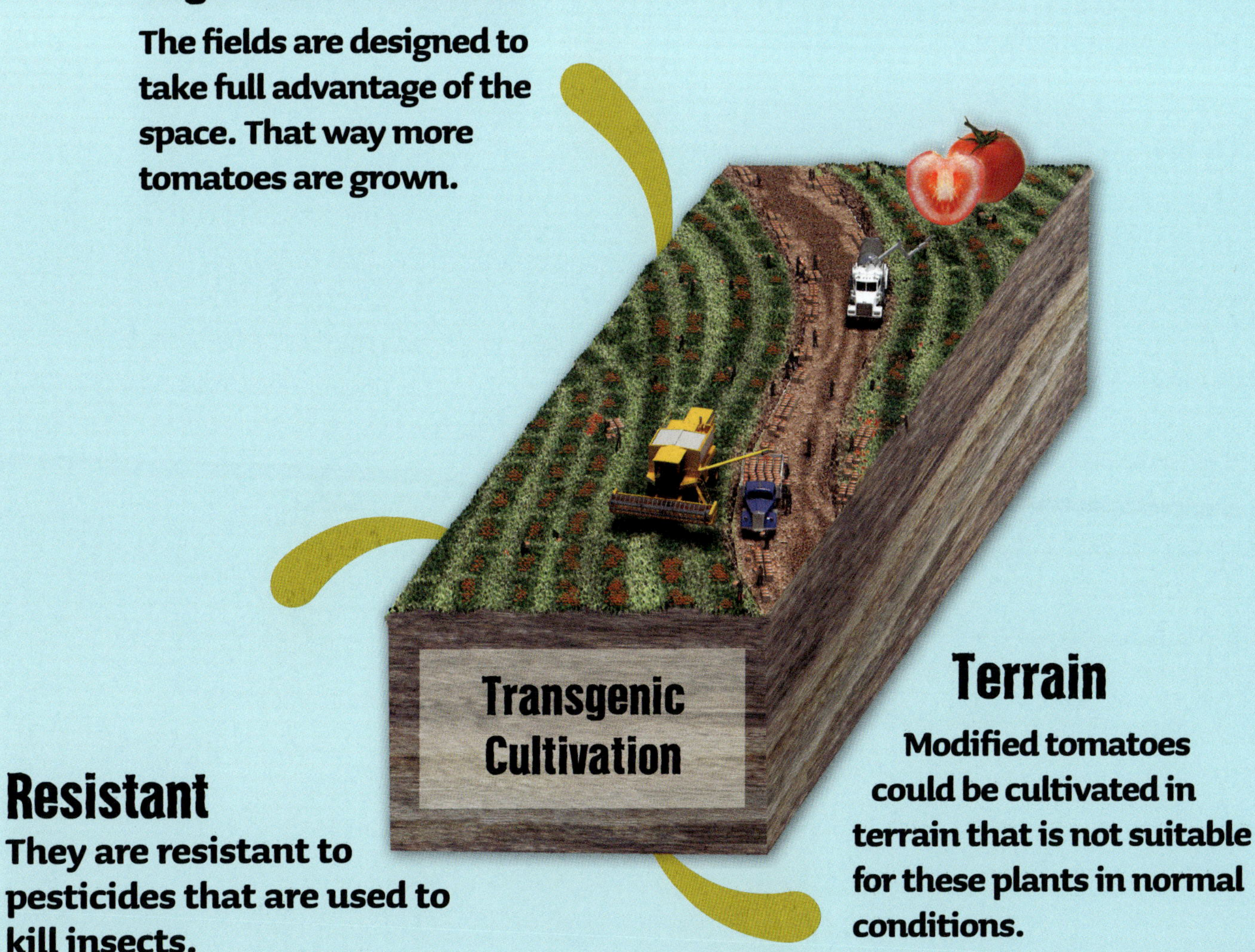

High Performance

The fields are designed to take full advantage of the space. That way more tomatoes are grown.

Terrain

Modified tomatoes could be cultivated in terrain that is not suitable for these plants in normal conditions.

Resistant

They are resistant to pesticides that are used to kill insects.

LABELS SPEAK VOLUMES

Consumers can see if a product has been produced in a sustainable way. These products have a label certified by an organization, which ensures that they meet environmental criteria.

Each Label Has a Meaning

These indicate that the product has been manufactured while respecting the environment.

Look for the Official Labels

These are granted by the official bodies of each country, and they are the most reliable.

Change by Country or Region

More than 84 countries have official eco-labels—for example, the European Union's flower or the Nordic swan.

PACKAGING IS IMPORTANT

Another thing that you should take into account when buying a product is whether its packaging is recyclable. Here are some symbols to help you recognize them.

Recyclable Aluminum

It is on packages and cans manufactured with recyclable aluminum.

Recyclable Materials

It indicates that the materials used to manufacture the product are recyclable. If it contains a percentage (for example, 70%), it means that only that part can be recycled.

Dispose of Each Thing in Its Container

This symbol reminds us that we should dispose or place the product in the appropriate bin or suitable site so that it can be recycled.

Waste Management

It informs us that the manufacturer takes part in waste management. It guarantees that the container will be recycled.

AVOID PLASTIC

Plastic is a versatile, efficient, and cheap material that has completely invaded our daily lives. At home, school, work, in the car ... anywhere we go, we find plastic objects. The problem is that it takes a long time for it to degrade when we dispose of it and it damages the environment. That is why it is important to reduce its consumption.

Biodegradable Alternative

There are plastics that are produced from vegetable materials, such as corn, wheat, or potatoes, that degrade naturally. Many supermarkets use these types of bags now.

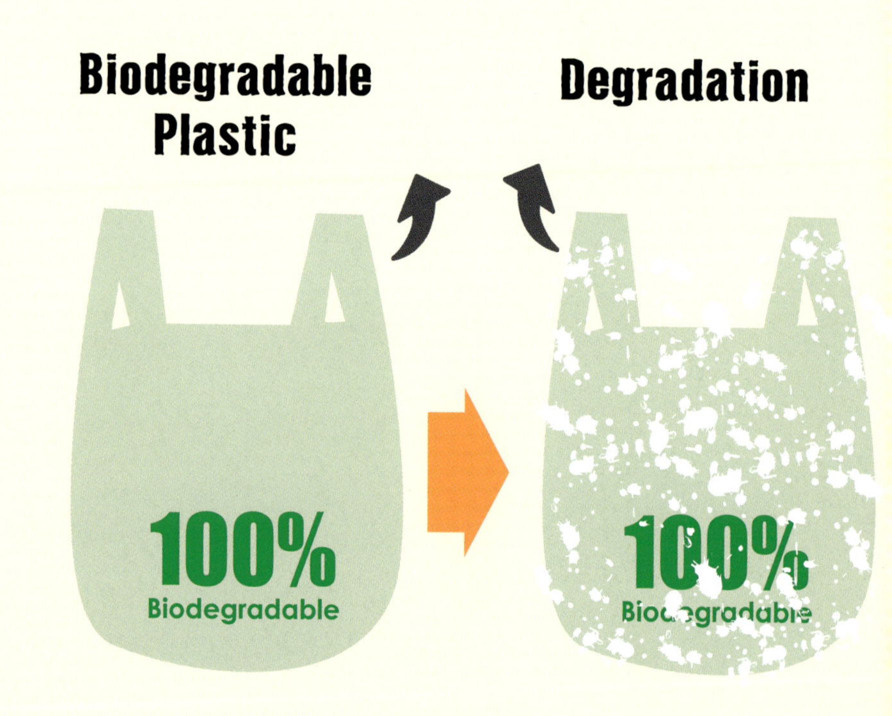

Difficult to Recycle

Another problem with plastic is that it is hard to recycle, which makes it even more harmful to the planet. Polystyrene and resin are the least recyclable materials.

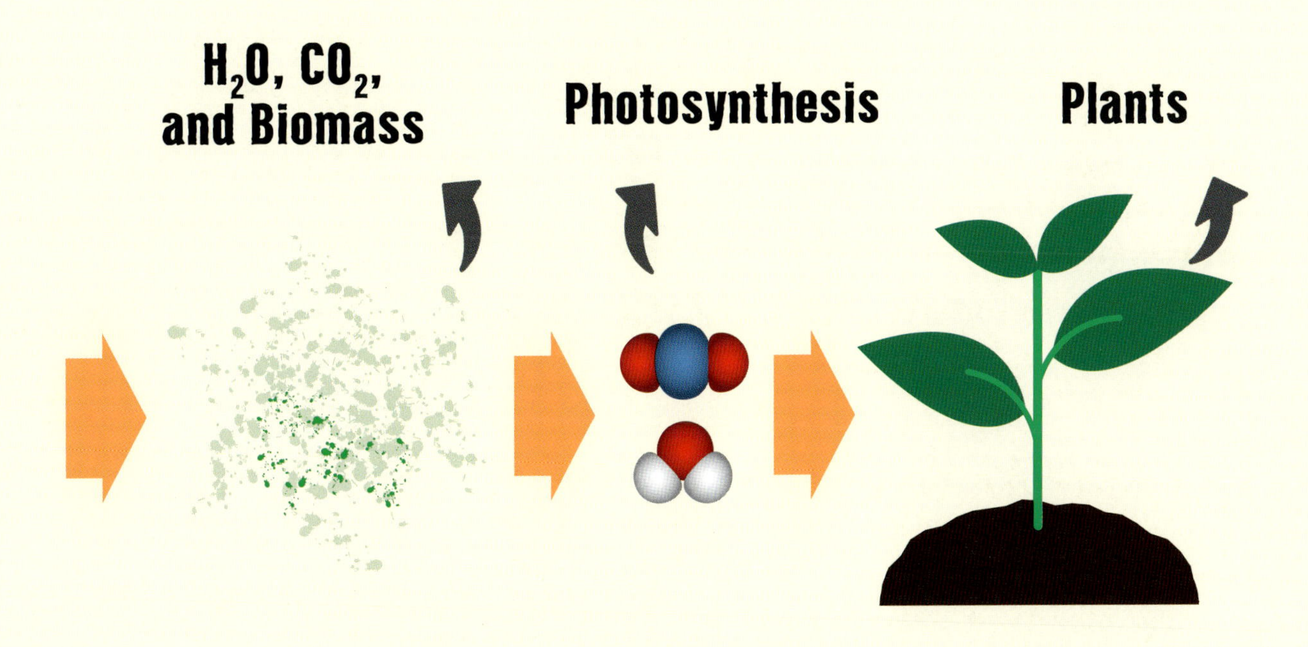

FAIR TRADE

Fair trade ensures that farmers and workers receive fair payment for their work, while also ensuring the care of nature. Take a look at the examples in the graphic.

Small Producers

A large part of fair trade derives from small farmers. Buying fair trade products helps improve the living conditions of these producers.

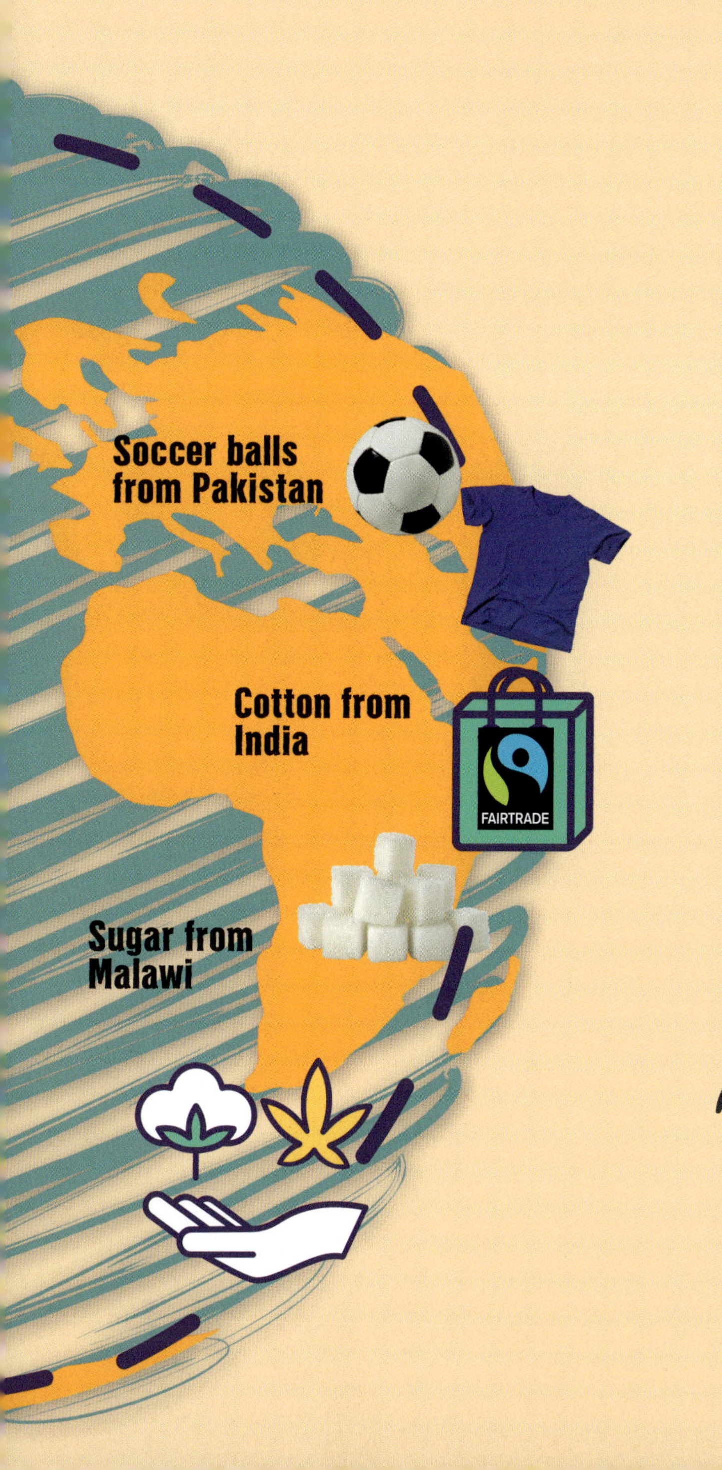

Fair Prices

Because fewer people are involved in the process, producers can get a fairer price for their products.

Look for the Seal

Fair trade products bear a seal that identifies them. It is necessary for a fair trade organization to certify it in order to obtain it.

Respect for the Environment

Fair trade also ensures that production is respectful of the environment.

SUSTAINABLE FASHION

Do you know that your clothes cost much more than what you paid for them? The fashion and clothing industry is one of the most polluting industries in the world. We must be aware of our clothing consumption and what we are buying.

Change the Model of Consumption

The current model of the clothing business is based on the fastest and cheapest method possible for volume and production. We buy a cheap item, we use it a few times, and then we throw it out. This is not a sustainble model for the environment.

Each Item Matters

Your shoes, your dress, your jeans... each article of clothing has a life cycle and an impact. We should try to get to know the full social and environmental impact, from cotton growing to the dyeing and manufacturing processes.

Recycling

Reusing clothes cuts down on complex industrial processes, contributes to water and energy conservation, and makes less waste.

WHICH CLOTHES ARE SUSTAINABLE?

Clothing can be made from many types of fabric, but not all are equally environmentally friendly. That is why it is important to read the label of a garment carefully before buying it and choose those that use more sustainable materials.

Organic Cotton

Organic cotton is better for the environment than regular cotton because it uses less water and it does not have involve harmful chemical products.

Sustainable Viscose

It is a natural and biodegradable material that comes from trees. It is important to make sure that it comes from forests that are well cared for.

Natural Dyes from Plants

Due to the chemical products used, fabric dyes are harmful to our environment. On the other hand, dyes that come from plants are completely natural and biodegradable. These are more expensive but they are safer for people's health.

Recycled Materials

Many companies have started to reuse fabrics that would normally become waste to recycle them into new fabrics. Recycled polyester and nylon, for example, are used to make fishing nets and carpet fibers.

SUITABLE TOYS

Toys that appear on television in advertising campaigns are not always the best ones nor the most environmentally conscious. There are many factors to take into account before choosing suitable toys.

Avoid Plastic and Batteries

Toys made with plastic and those that use batteries are the least sustainable.

Toys should have a seal on the label or on the box that certifies that they are safe.

Check Age of Use

Each toy is designed for a particular age group, which should be indicated on the package.

Seal of Quality

Educational toys are a fun way to teach important concepts. These toys can be passed on from person to person to spread knowledge!

Better Education

If possible, we should recycle, give away, or exchange a toy before throwing it out and buying a new one.

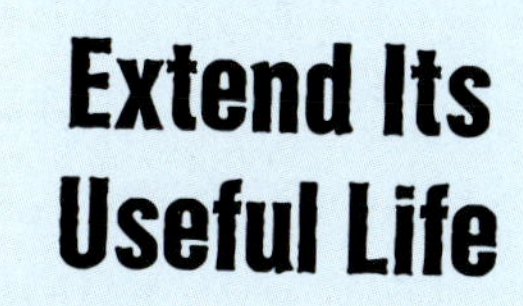

Extend Its Useful Life

RESPONSIBLE CONSUMPTION

The Five Ecological R's

Reduce, repurpose, repair, reuse, and recycle. Remember these words before getting rid of an item and buying a new one. Less waste means less pollution.

Local Products

Select products that are produced or manufactured close to where you live. That way you will reduce the amount of fuel that will be needed to transport them. And remember: avoid plastic bags and containers.

Whenever possible, you should always choose eco-friendly products. In doing so, you will help keep the planet healthy when you shop!

If You Don't Need It, Please Don't Buy It

Making a list of our needs before leaving home will help us avoid buying the first thing we see at the store.

MAKE YOUR OWN SOAP

In this experiment you will learn how to make soap with natural ingredients.

YOU WILL NEED:
- Soap flakes
- Microwave-safe bowl or an old pot
- Glycerin
- Rubbing alcohol
- Cinnamon or paprika
- Small molds

STEP BY STEP: Find the instructions on the next page!

STEP ONE

Place 1 cup of soap flakes in a pot or bowl. Add 1/3 cup of glycerin and 2 teaspoons of alcohol.

STEP TWO

Carefully add 1/8 cup water to the mixture and stir.

STEP THREE

Add 1 teaspoon of cinnamon to the mixture and 1 teaspoon of paprika if you want to add color.

STEP FOUR

Heat up the mixture on the stove or in the microwave until it boils.

STEP FIVE

As soon as the mixture boils, remove it from the heat, stirring continuously.

Once the mixture has cooled down and is transparent but still liquid, pour it in molds and wait for it to harden.

STEP SIX

Conclusion

The soap is very soft and will not irritate the skin because its ingredients are natural.

Glossary

biodegradable: able to be broken down by the action of living organisms such as bacteria

certified: recognized as having met special qualifications or standards

consumption: the act or process of using goods

environment: the conditions that surround a living thing and affect the way it lives; the natural world in which a plant or animal lives

manufactured: made by machine in a large quantity

natural resources: things in nature that can be used by people

production: the process of making or growing something to sell it

sustainable: capable of continuing or being kept up over time

Index

aluminum, 8, 22
biodegradable plastic, 24
biodiversity, 17
ecological backpack, 10–11, 12–13
environment, 7, 11, 12, 14, 27, 28
fair trade, 26–27
organic, 14
packaging, 15, 22, 23
plastic, 24–25, 32, 34
recycling, 8, 10, 22, 23, 25, 31, 33, 34
transgenic food, 16–17, 19